Tickner's Ponies

John Tickner
Tickner's Ponies

Written and illustrated by

John Tickner

° THE °
SPORTSMAN'S
PRESS
LONDON

First published in 1966
Reprinted by The Sportsman's Press in 1991

© John Tickner 1991

British Library Cataloguing in Publication Data
Tickner, John *1913–*
  Tickner's ponies.
  1. Livestock. Ponies
  I. Title
  636.16
    ISBN 0–948253–44–4

Printed in Great Britain by The Bath Press, Avon

Contents

Introduction

THE average modern human's introduction to the world of horses and horsemanship is by way of ponies.

The man or woman who achieves success and fame by taking part in internationally popular equestrian events such as show-jumping, the Grand National and dressage and cross-country trials, almost certainly began his or her career with a pony at a local gymkhana or other activity of the Pony Club.

The British pony, of which there are a number of distinct breeds whose histories go back many centuries and whose modern representatives are highly prized throughout the world, has done much to improve the standard of British horsemanship. It has also done much to preserve the British horseman's well-known sense of humour. The pony often seems to have a peculiarly wicked sense of humour of its own and without one no horse person could possibly get along with the little beasts. As it is they can make perfect companions and ideal sporting partners.

This book, the result of much painful research, is being re-published because it is apparently, much approved of by ponies and pony persons of all types, ages and sizes.

John Tickner
Westhide, Hereford

1. Early Ponies

It must have been the ponies who started the whole business of pulling the legs of humans. In the course of time, when horses came along, they, too, got the idea of the fun of the thing and so for many centuries the equine race has been neighing its head off with laughter at the thought that it has succeeded in making the human race pet it and clothe it and feed it and generally toil day and night to keep it in comfort. And horses and ponies have done this by the simple means of letting humans think that they, the horses and ponies, are their faithful servants!

It would be so convenient to bundle it into a rabbit hutch

It is true, of course, that once upon a time, long, long ago, humans did not wait upon horses and ponies hand and hoof. Instead, in the days when all horses were pony-size and even smaller, living wildly and shaggily in wild and shaggy parts of the world, they were chased about by Man's ancestors for the purpose of being turned into pony stews; but ponies do not wish to be reminded about that and nor do most humans. Today, the situation is almost entirely reversed, particularly in Britain where ponies are much more likely to be the ones to take the first bite. Sometimes they can even be seen chasing pony people about, just to remind them that the situation *has* been reversed and all because of the great intelligence of the pony race in establishing its supremacy.

No one can be quite sure what the earliest ponies looked like. It has been said that the very earliest of them all were so small that they bore little resemblance to the pony as we know it today and some pony people have had cause to regret that they ever got any bigger; it would be so convenient to pick up a really nasty-minded pony when it was having one of its temperaments and bundle it into a rabbit hutch. It is probable that when, a few centuries later, the creatures began to get a bit larger, they looked something like big hairy guinea pigs, with large teeth just showing through the whiskers, and small hoofs. Of course they've changed quite considerably since then—well, some of them have.

What is condescendingly referred to by pony people as the Domestication of the Pony was in reality the Domestication of the Pony Person by the Pony. It began by the ponies deciding that they had been out in the cold long enough, or the heat, according to whether they were living in cold or hot climates at the time of decision. 'Let us,' they said, at their ponies' club meetings, 'cease to be obviously creatures of the wild and move in on Man. Once we have moved in,' they said, 'we can continue to be as wild as we like, but only when we feel like it and in the greatest possible man-made comfort.' The motion, unlike many of the resolutions put to pony club meetings today, was undoubtedly carried unanimously and so ponies duly moved in on Man in the most polite, not to say smoothy, sort of way.

All over the pony-populated world, humans, sitting before their fires in their caves or fanning themselves in their grass huts, were surprised to find shaggy ponies drifting daintily into their abodes, fluttering their long eyelashes and looking as if buttered carrots wouldn't melt in their mouths. When they—the humans—had been persuaded to come down from the highest points in their caves and huts to which they had naturally nipped as soon as they had gathered their wits, the greatest take-over in history had been accomplished; Pony had taken over Man and there is every indication that Pony will continue to hang on to Man, physically and spiritually, until the end of time.

There is plenty of evidence on the walls of caves that ponies were accepted as suitable subjects for the popular art of the period, and the vague shapes of humans, impressed upon the rock, may be

An archeologist's sinister discovery

accepted as evidence that Early Pony was capable of kicking people it didn't like as hard and as far as Modern Pony can. An archeologist recently discovered that the pony designs on cave walls were painted on, but (and this is the sinister bit!) the spread-eagled designs of humans could be *peeled off*.

And so ponies, having taken over humans, had to decide the best way to make use of them without having to overwork themselves. It is not generally known that there is a Pony Trade Union, but the people who are accepted by ponies as almost 'One of Them' will at least have heard a whisper to the effect that the little four-legged darlings agreed among themselves, centuries ago, that the secret slogan should be 'The Pony is always right but the owner should always appear to be right'.

Now this might well be thought, by non-pony persons, to be a reason for getting rid of not only ponies but also pony persons. This is a most reasonable and logical idea, especially at Christmas or birthday times, the occasions when the Pony is apt to insinuate itself into the most unlikely homes; but, it is only fair to warn non-pony persons, especially those who have daughters, that the pony will always win. If you cannot afford a pony for yourself,

11

someone will give you one they also cannot afford, or which has frightened them into giving it away.

But to go back to the early days of the Pony Take-over. Having convinced humans that they were much more useful as household pets than as beasts of the chase, they had the sense to realise that they would have to show at least a little interest in work. They therefore permitted themselves to be used in chariots, or as sawn-off cavalry horses in cavalry charges. That wasn't too bad a life at all for those really intelligent members of the pony tribe who had the sense to stop short before they became involved in the business of Man being beastly to Man at close quarters. Those ponies who

The sense to stop short

were stupid and arrogant enough to let their families grow taller, so that they finally grew into what are now known as horses, got what they deserved—a lot of hard work. The more intelligent pony strains stayed small and, although some of them were cunningly tricked by Man into carrying quite heavy weights, such as lead, wool, fuel and food and even, one regrets to have to record, contraband (the story of ghostly horsemen, which frightened ancient villagers so much that they dared not look out of their cottage windows at night when they heard the patter of tiny hoofs, was undoubtedly thought up by some wicked pony in order to get an extra ration of brandy with his oats) the majority of British ponies stopped carrying heavy weights about years ago. There is even a theory that the internal combustion engine was invented by a pony but, whether that is true or not, the fact is that ponies, with the exception of a few backward Abroad types, have achieved their ambition and now spend most of their time eating, drinking and sleeping and, when they feel so inclined, taking exercise by carrying humans around and getting rid of them when they feel too heavy.

It is almost impossible for a human, whether young, or a Mum or Dad, to get rid of a pony unless the pony itself wishes to change ownership, but we recently came across something in a book, written by a distinguished horse person many years ago, which gives a glimpse of hope to unwilling pony persons, especially unwilling Mum and Dad pony-owners. 'Horses,' wrote this expert, 'attain their greatest height in temperate climates and diminish in size in cold climates and also in hot ones'. If therefore, you are troubled by a pony you have innocently acquired, stolen, or had thrust upon you, especially if it is a nasty big one, all you have to do is to take it on your next expedition to the frozen North or on your next trip to the Equator and, with luck, it will either diminish in size sufficiently to become manageable or, with even more luck, melt or freeze away entirely.

13

2. Pony Breeds

BEFORE YOU have anything to do with ponies at close quarters it is advisable to learn all about the different breeds of ponies. Before you go anywhere near a real, experienced Pony Person, it is essential. It can be most embarrassing to talk at length about ponies to a person who is a New Forest enthusiast, for example, when all you know is that the little hairy ones are Shetlands, you think.

We are aware, of course, as you must also pretend to be if you want to get anywhere in the equestrian world, that there are many kinds of ponies, in countries as far apart as Iceland and Africa and Asia, but, having had some nasty experiences with Abroad ponies in our time, we will confine ourselves to the little creatures of our own country with which, on reflection, we have also had the occasional alarming encounter. However, it must be stressed, in the interests of the livestock export business and with an eye on wealthy visitors from Abroad, that the British Native Pony Breeds are absolutely unbeatable. For one thing the British wouldn't allow it and, for another, nor would the ponies.

The first thing that the beginner in the pony world must learn, if he or she is to be accepted into the chatty social circle of experts which is a recognised part of every horse and pony show, is that every British Native Pony, whatever the breed, has perfect manners and will carry anyone or anything all day, will jump a house and will pull a variety of carriages. This is especially true if one is breeding and selling the little dears. The person who is only just entering the sacred circle of the pony world is likely to be regarded as, at the worst, harmless, and, at the best, intelligent, if he or she bears this general principle in mind.

But one will never get far in the pony world by just standing around at the edge of a group, smiling and neighing a little at what one thinks are the appropriate moments and being regarded as either harmless or merely intelligent. If one stays at that phase one will be sold a dud sooner or later and one will never learn how to sell ponies oneself. And so, if one wants to get on, one absolutely must learn, not only how to tell one breed of pony from another, but also how to tell one group of pony breeders from another. Here, then, is a brief description, with background information, of the British Native Pony breeds.

15

The Highland. It is reasonable, and also advisable, to start the list with the Highland because it is the largest and, in its own opinion, as well as in the opinion of the Highlanders who breed it, the strongest of all our native breeds of ponies. It is advisable to put it at the top of the list because the Highlanders, if not the tallest, are, in their own opinion and in the opinion of various other breeds who have had the misfortune to fall out with them, the toughest of the humans we breed in these Islands. Englishmen, Irishmen and Welshmen who may have started to read this book are requested not to throw it away at this stage as we have things to say about them later.

There are, it is accepted by most Highlanders, two types of Highland ponies in existence today: the Western Islands pony and the rather heftier Mainland variety. Several hundred years B.C. the Celts had been sufficiently domesticated by ponies to look after them and not just to regard them as a nice change from venison as a Sunday joint, but there have been found, in the former homes of Scottish cavemen, the remains of ponies which, we hardly dare mention, may have been used as ingredients for the ancestor of the haggis. On no account must you mention this yourself, especially

Highland Ponies think nothing of carrying twenty stone

16

in a Highland place of alcoholic refreshment or in one of those restaurants where today they, quite rightly, pride themselves on the superlative quality of Scottish beef.

Highland ponies have, for many years, lent a more or less willing hoof on the small Scottish farms in return for oats and comfort and, even today, with tractors moving into what were once stables, they have refused to move out entirely and fend for themselves on the mountains. Instead, they stroll up and down the slopes, admiring the scenery and carrying dead deer about, as well as consenting, in return for extra rations, to carry elderly shooting people up the rough places which are bad for elderly people's shooting ability if they walk. Highland ponies think nothing of carrying 20 stone, it is said, but the look on the faces of some Highland ponies when carrying 20 stone elderly sportsmen gives a keen observer the impression that they are thinking about it very deeply indeed. Characteristics of the Scottish ponies are a head set on a powerful neck, large bright eyes, good girth, sturdy limbs and a short back. There is a theory that ponies tend to look like the people they live among—or is it the other way round?

The Shetland. The Shetland or 'Sheltie' is the smallest of all the British pony breeds and in its natural, unclipped state, is covered all over with hair, mane and tail. It has neat little hoofs, neat little eyes somewhere inside its long shaggy front fringe, neat little legs and great big teeth which emerge unexpectedly from all that hair to grab anything it takes a fancy to and humans it doesn't. It is enormously strong, as anyone who tries to tug it in a direction which it has no intention of going soon finds out, and for centuries was used for carrying just about everything and everybody about the Islands. Shetlands, however, never have been and never will be slaves and they are still quite capable of dropping everything, including humans, without notice, if they are not treated with the greatest respect. If handled extremely politely they make very nice pets of people.

These little Early Britons—nobody knows when they first arrived and they have never been persuaded to tell even other ponies—have one weakness of which a clever owner can take advantage, and that is vanity. They are obviously delighted when humans go all twee about them and remark to each other how sweet Shetlands are and what fun it would be to be owned by one and how dignified they are in the Show Ring and so on.

What makes them smile with delight and pride more than anything is the applause they receive when they are led around the ring in the leading rein classes or, even better, when they are

17

The Shetland Pony is enormously strong

drawing a tiny carriage. As these shows are held in the summer when the Shelties are not as hairy as they are in the winter, it is often possible to see the smile of satisfaction on their tiny faces. But, if you suddenly find yourself owned by a Shetland, do not make the mistake of assuming that it is a sloppy, sentimental kind of pony which will let you do just as you like. Some people who thought this have carried tiny, twee hoof-prints to prove how wrong they were, all their lives. It must be mentioned that Shetlands live to a very great age and many of them outlive the humans they have taken over. There is nothing sinister about this fact, so far as we know.

The Welsh. Ponies of the Welsh types are rather more tricky creatures to discuss than most other ponies for several reasons, among which are that not only are there several officially-recognised different sorts of Welsh native ponies but that Welshmen and Welshwomen are either likely to become offended, if you happen to praise the wrong sort, or to burst into song in favour of the kind they insist is the really original Welsh pony. Either experience can be unnerving, according to the temperament or ear for music of the listener.

18

But, whatever the claims of the champions of other breeds, it seems to have been established indeed that the Welsh ponies have the longest-known history. It is claimed that they were on singing terms with the Romans and there is proof that they had considerable influence on the Welsh poets, on a number of whom they

Early Welsh Pony and Early Welsh poet

left their distinctive mark. A few of the early Welsh poets were literally carried away by the early Welsh ponies, so overcome were they by their beauty. It is also said that the majority of Welsh poets were much better at Welsh poetry than they were at Welsh horsemanship.

You will be told that the Welsh ponies of today consist of the Welsh Mountain Pony, the Welsh Pony and the Welsh Cob, according to which part of Wales you are in or which show you are at. Whichever you are in or at, it is advisable to agree with whatever you are being told about, or it is trouble you will be in. The Modern Welsh Mountain Pony does very nicely indeed at the Shows, and the Welsh Cob, which claims that about six hundred years or so ago it was well-known as an all-round mount for knights in armour and was accustomed to carry out any amount of duties, from rescuing all-round damsels in distress from all-round wicked

19

barons to taking part in all-round tournaments and rather long-drawn-out crusades, is in demand still, although for less exciting activities.

Dales and Fells. Once upon a time, Dales and Fells ponies belonged to the same pony family, living in the North of England, the only difference being that the Dales lived on the east side while the Fells lived on the west.

In those days the Dales and the Fells not only looked alike but were all closely related and spoke the same language, with slightly different accents and dialects, of course, and, according to people who should know, they claimed an ancestry which went back to the

Roman ancestor of the Dales and Fells Ponies

horses which had consented to carry Roman cavalry about the Roman Wall. Some of those Romans must have had an irritating time trying to climb up the wall after being bucked off, being laughed at and shot at with bows and arrows by the Picts and the Scots all the time and then, when they got to the top again, having to pursue their ponies all along Hadrian's masterpiece, which went

20

on for miles and miles. Incidentally, it seems almost impossible to keep the Romans out of British pony history.

In more recent times, the Dales and the Fells, like the majority of good families, decided to marry into other families, the former developing a liking for rather heavier-type mates and so becoming the slightly larger of the two branches, physically. Both branches of the family, now regarded as separate, are famous for their ability to carry great weights and at one time were to be seen, not only doing all kinds of jobs on the farms, but also acting as pack ponies lugging great lumps of lead for miles. It might be thought that they were not very bright to take on such employment but, on the other hand, it must have been tremendous fun to drop a lump of lead on a human's toe and listen to the results. Today, unfortunately, there are not a large number of Dales and Fells about, but those who are still about have given up carrying some 16 stone of lead around and instead, carry some 16 stone of farmer out hunting. The wisest of them concentrate on taking part in pony shows and watch their owners carrying some 16 stone of trophies home.

Dartmoor. This is an ancient moorland breed which once ran about the moors of South Devon in Herds, minding its own business. Dartmoor has been described by enterprising and imaginative tourist agencies as a 'rugged place dotted with fallen rocks'. There are legends, oft told in the ancient inns of the moor, especially when there are dotty-looking visitors from the towns within earshot, which imply that the fallen rocks were early dotty-type tourists who thought that the Dartmoor ponies they had hired from what they thought were dotty locals were as stupid as they tried to look. The ponies, assisted by the pixies, they do tell you, got rid of the early tourists who didn't believe the genuineness of Dartmoor ponies, or Dartmoor pixies, by bucking them off and leaving them absolutely and literally petrified. The Dartmoor ponies have been much spoilt from time to time by the introduction of the wrong sort of cross-breeding. There have, however, in recent years, been successful attempts on the part of a few enthusiasts to establish a good type. This cannot entirely be said, according to local opinion, of all the tourists. The pixies, it is locally agreed, have remained pure.

The Exmoor. The Exmoor pony, anyone who lives on Exmoor, particularly those who breed them, will tell you, is the oldest of the British pony breeds and they will add, if they have read their Exmoor pony history pamphlets properly, this little beast—the word is used in the nicest and literal sense—was kicking people

21

around in Britain before the Romans came. Whatever else it may not have done (Exmoor ponies have probably done most things in their time) we can take our horse-persons-type hats off to it for having beaten those Romans at kicking people around in Britain. It is likely that the original Exmoor pony even kicked Romans.

New Forest. There were wild ponies in the New Forest before the Normans came and, it is thought, at one time the forest ponies and those on the moors were closely related, but as the New Forest became fashionable as a top-class hunting area it was inevitable that, sooner or later, the breeding in it would be improved. And so, whether they liked it or not, the ponies had better breeding thrust upon them, according to the ideas of the enthusiasts of the various other pony breeds in existence. Even when the forest had ceased to be a Royal hunting ground, the ponies still had better breeding introduced, so much so that at one stage in the history of New Forest ponies, it is said by ancient verderers, (who are, as everyone who knows about forests must be aware, the people who look after the place and pick up all that litter and stuff on Monday mornings) the ponies could be heard neighing in Welsh and Arabic, as well as Scottish, Devonian and North Country accents. Some of

New Forest Pony enjoying picnic

them, it is said, had decidedly Thoroughbred voices. Naturally enough, they grew in all sizes and colours, but in recent years, they have been so much improved all over again that they are now not only looking like improved New Forest ponies but are beginning to neigh in genuine New Forest accents again.

For many years New Forest ponies have been having fun playing 'last across the road is chicken' in front of the cars of holiday motorists. As this was tending not only to reduce the numbers of motorists but also of ponies, the Authorities have done something about it by putting up fences and it won't be long before the only fun the ponies will get will be shouting rude forest remarks at the motorists through the wire. They will continue to indulge in their favourite game of sneaking up on picnic parties in the depths of the woods and pinching their cucumber sandwiches, of course, but this has been an undisputed right of the ponies since the Norman kings had picnics there.

Connemara. The Irish have known all about ponies ever since there were Irish and Irish ponies, and no honest Irish horse-dealer will mind us mentioning that much legend and myth has been associated, not only with their country but also with their dealings.

It is said that St. Patrick himself was an enthusiastic horse-person, but there are no records to prove whether he sold ponies to the early Irish or whether they sold them to him, or whether the leprechauns started it all. But the fact that nobody knows more about horse-dealing than an Irishman remains undisputed, especially by those who have bought horses or ponies in Ireland. Nearly all Irish horses and ponies can do almost anything, even when they are not expected to do it, and the Connemara has accomplished most things in its time, from being a family pony, all wreathed in smiles and carrying a smiling Irish family, to playing polo, doing dressage and hunting anything from foxes to people.

It should be clear to the discerning reader that all British Native Ponies are excellent in every way but some are much better than others. This might be thought to be impossible, but if you talk to the top people in organisations which concentrate upon improving all the breeds you will find it is perfectly true. If you take one of the officials, who has been telling you how wonderul they all are, aside and out of earshot of the others, you will discover that a particular breed is the only one that is superb, has never been ruined by bad foreign blood, is worth paying a lot of money to obtain and, by coincidence, happens to be the breed that he—or more often she—is busily breeding.

Irish ponies can do almost anything

3. Ponycraft

BEFORE any young person can regard himself or herself as a real pony person, he or she must acquire what is known by the initiated as Ponycraft. This word is often spoken in a hushed voice by expert pony folk when talking in front of beginners and no doubt you will do the same when you have achieved Ponycraft. But, meanwhile, do not be frightened of it. Reduced to its simplest terms, Ponycraft is only the art of being as crafty as a pony, which is the best you can possibly do because nobody has yet succeeded in being craftier than any pony that ever was born.

Even the dottiest beginner will appreciate that, in order to acquire Ponycraft, it is necessary to make the close acquaintance of ponies. Admittedly, this can be a frightening experience until you learn that, despite all those teeth and hoofs, ponies want to be loved by humans. This may sound a bit 'twee' and sentimental, but the awful truth is that they want to be loved in order to get large helpings of oats and hay and grass and carrots. As soon as you realise this, you will be able to get on with ponies quite well and they will even let you feed them and eventually, if you are very cunning, sit on their backs now and again.

If you cannot persuade your parents to buy you a pony as soon as you think you need one, you should go to a riding school and get your parents to pay for you to ride one of its. Incidentally, it is worth mentioning at this stage that it is advisable to go to a riding school whether you have your own pony or not, although many young would-be pony people think that they can teach themselves, and even more parents think that they should, too, in order to save the instruction fees. That is one reason why some young people don't live long enough to grow up to be horse people.

By the way, thanks largely to the British Horse Society, which is the top horse and pony organisation of Britain, most riding schools are now highly respectable and absolutely All Right, and so Daddy and Mummy have no excuse for not sending their kiddy-winkies for highly respectable instruction to officially approved schools, which is how things should be. The complicated business of learning to ride a pony which, as all the modern and highly respectable riding instructors will tell you, is very simple once you know how, has been dealt with by so many expert writers of books that we have no intention of going into it all over again. It is, therefore, assumed that you have at least a vague idea about what

The mucking-out stage

you should do to get your pony going in the required direction at the expected moment. It is also assumed that you can get on to the thing in the first place.

Having learned something of the rudiments of riding, you must concentrate upon this most important close-acquaintance and, as the more sentimental female pony persons might put it, 'soul-mate' kind of association with your little four-footed friends—you hope. This is the first step in Ponycraft. The second stage in Ponycraft is persuading your parents that you really do need your own pony, especially if they have sent you to the afore-mentioned respectable riding school in the hope that you would have lost your nerve during the mucking-out-of-stables stage.

But let us assume that you have won through to the getting-your-own pony stage and all you have to do now is to select the pony which will be your very own with which you will be able to get very closely acquainted, until you get fed up with each other. The next step is to find the right type of pony and, of course, the riding school you have been attending will be able to advise parents about the type most suitable for you, without any bias at all, it must be added, especially if they happen to have just the sort in the stables at that very moment.

It is only fair, in the interests of both young riders and parents, to introduce here some advice on the types of pony to consider as

Has the pony been accustomed to carrying a child?

possible purchases. In the first place, both parents and young must ask themselves, when presented with a likely animal by a likely pony seller, 'Has the pony been accustomed to carrying a child?' The best way to test this is by offering it a child. Any that happen to be standing around at the time will do.

If the pony carries it about with its teeth it must be regarded as unreliable and even those with soft mouths would be more suitable in gundog trials than in the pony world. The pony is meant to carry the child on its back. If the pony allows the young person to stay upright on its back for a reasonable period, it can be assumed that it has the right idea. If it has a kind eye, a smile on its face, and a tendency to go to sleep, it is probably just the right sort for the beginner-pony-owners to learn with and to discover that few things in the pony world, ponies and those who buy and sell them in particular, are what they seem. It has been said that the best way to acquire a pony is from a friend rather than from a dealer. It depends whether you want to keep your friends or not.

Having acquired what you think is the right sort of pony, the young owner must pursue the art of Ponycraft by spending as much time as possible with it, this being very important if he or she is supposed to be riding it at the time. The young owner must get to know its temperament, its wants and unwants, its loves and hates, its worries and average state of neurosis, pony and horse psychology being a most significant part of Ponycraft today.

For example, if the dear little beast takes to bucking its rider off at frequent intervals, taking bites out of people's arms and breeches and showing a general tendency to have an odd sense of humour, modern, enlightened pony-thought suggests that *you* are to blame and that you are failing in your Ponycraft. There are pony-people psychologists who go as far as inferring that if you wish to get to know your pony really well you should take a tip from the pony people of ancient Arabia and sleep in the pony's bedroom. It is unlikely that the modern European or Western kind of parent will allow the pony to sleep in a European or Western kind of bedroom, however devoted they may be to their children or their children's ponies. Any young pony person who succeeds in persuading them to do so will indeed have achieved the ultimate in Ponycraft, at any rate from the pony's point of view.

But you will find that the longer you are associated with ponies the more you have to learn about Ponycraft. Even the people who reach the top of the Horse World and think they know all about Horsecraft and Ponycraft, are apt to discover, when they come into close association with ponies again, on such occasions as demonstrating to nieces how they used to ride Abroad ponies in the Old

Days, that they have forgotten a few tiny details about Ponycraft
– the ones that ponies never forget.

They discover they have forgotten a few details about Ponycraft

4.Crafty Ponies

ALL MEMBERS of the horse family are intelligent, have a keen sense of smell, excellent hearing, good eyesight and a remarkable amount of insight. Ponies have all these attributes, only rather more so than their bigger brethren. British Native Ponies have an additional method of self-defence—a keen sense of humour which not all pony-owners, including some of the British ones who have had British Native Ponies inflicted upon them, always appreciate. For the sake of simplification and in order to explain the basic principles of pony psychology to both those humans who do, and those who do not, regard being bucked off, chased round a field, bitten or deposited in a ditch, as screamingly funny, we will call it just plain pony craftiness. It is advisable to assume, when you are just getting acquainted with the pony world, that all ponies are crafty and that some ponies are craftier than others.

For the benefit of those who have not already found out for themselves, here is a brief list of crafty ponies into which you should be able to fit yours without much hesitation. If your pony does not correspond to at least one of the types, it is either not a pony at all or is that long-sought paragon, the Ideal Pony, in which case it could be sold to a zoological society for an enormous sum as the only specimen of its kind in existence, whatever the advertisements in the top horse and pony publications may say. The average pony owner will be able to fit their own little beasty into several of the following categories, unless of course, it has been put up for sale.

Angel-face. This crafty little darling is usually very small, with lots of hair and great big soulful eyes with which it gazes dreamily at the world. It has a soppy sort of smile on its face, nuzzles everyone in an affectionate way and positively beams when people who don't know much about ponies say 'Aw!' and go into ecstasies about its cuddliness.

It is easily caught, in fact it gives itself up, and allows itself to be saddled and bridled and even mounted without any resentment. It carries its rider dreamily along for a quarter of a mile and then stops and gazes angelically and dreamily upon life as it passes it by. It has such a sweet nature that it declines to move farther into the sinful world and is content to remain where it has decided to

31

It 'won't do anything'

stop, thinking lovely thoughts and picking wild flowers from the side of the lane. It is always sold as a 'patent safety' which it is, and the purchaser is always told that it 'won't do anything', which it won't—apart from remaining maddeningly and craftily angelic, and eating, of course. This type is worth its weight in gold for pony people who don't want to do anything. It usually manages to remain a family pet for the whole of its long life.

Exploring Type. A very crafty type of pony indeed; successful in getting out of any sort of enclosure and obtaining free meals from other people's fields and hay stores. It is too crafty to be observed studying the weak places in fences but, instead, pretends to be grazing in any new pasture into which it has just been turned while it is craftily watching, beneath its long eye-lashes, its owner carefully examining the spots it might use as an exit. As soon as it sees the owner looking worried and throwing bits of old branches into a gap, or fixing pieces of rusty wire above an ancient bit of timber, it makes a mental note to have a close look as soon as all humans are out of sight. Sure enough, it discovers, usually during the night, that the owner's fears were fully justified and it spends a happy hour or so exploring next door, taking its toll and leaving its signature before nipping smartly back, to be found dozing peacefully when its owner comes to ask in the morning whether it has been happy or not. The exploring type is particularly un-

Makes a mental note to have a close look

popular with next-door people who have beautiful gardens, standing crops and accessible supplies of pony fodder which was not intended to be pony fodder.

Get-'em-out-of-bed Type. This is a variation of the Exploring Type but is much nastier. It is not content to let itself out quietly and roam about other people's property without disturbing anyone. On the contrary, its object is to create as much disturbance as possible at a carefully-chosen time when its little game is likely to annoy as many humans as it can. Its method is to wait until the small hours on a very dark night and, having previously studied the weak places in the fences, on the same lines as the Exploring Type, it gets out, but as noisily as possible, finds the nearest hard road and canters up and down, neighing from time to time to imply that it is in dire distress and keeping an eye on all the bedroom windows within eyeshot. As soon as it is satisfied that all but the deaf or incurably lazy humans within earshot are out of bed, it lurks in the shadows until front doors open. With a squeal of delight it proceeds to dash past the nearest emerging human and clatters off into the darkness. As soon as it has gone round the nearest corner it lurks again, giggling to itself and watching the humans groping about and falling over each other. It has a lot of fun if it only does this

33

close to the home of its owners, but it gets much more pleasure if its owners live some distance away.

In the latter case it can enjoy listening to the nearest resident ringing up its owners and telling them to come over and collect their pet. It might be thought that Get-'Em-Out-Of-Bed type of ponies are not crafty at all, but they are. Not only do they have a lot of fun but they usually succeed in getting extra rations, because their owners conclude that the poor little beast only gets out because the grass is not good enough for it.

The Get-'em-out-of-bed type

Hard-to-get Type. Many ponies pretend to be hard to catch, just on principle, but the majority of them give themselves up after a short time and there is no craft in that. The pony who specialises in not being caught is a very different animal. He has developed the whole business into a major form of craftiness and the older he gets the better he becomes at it. The genuinely hard-to-get pony never reveals his skill when you first acquire him. He makes a point of coming to your call if you have him in your own paddock for a trial period before buying him, expecially if he thinks he is likely to have an easier time putting up with you as an owner than he did with the last lot.

It may not be until a month after the cheque has been signed by

He makes a point of coming to your call

kindly, or bullied, parents that the craftiness becomes apparent. Thereafter you will spend many happy hours, running around on the grass, making stranger and stranger noises, while the pony keeps just, but only just, out of range. Don't be depressed; think of the exercise you are getting and the valuable lessons in Ponycraft that you are learning. Hard-to-get type of ponies tend to have a lot of different owners—but they also have lots of fun.

Bolting Type. This kind is usually sold as a good hunter or trials pony, capable of taking on any obstacle; a pony with speed and stamina. It is often, quite accurately described as ignoring traffic and usually ignores traffic lights as well. The crafty thing about the bolter is that he or she only bolts towards home and comfort and never, never, in the direction of more work.

The All-round Crafty Pony. A rather rare specimen these days, you might think. It is the type that never displays any vice that you would care to admit it had. It is so crafty that it makes a point of being the Perfect Pony in front of people who matter. Its manners are impeccable at the Meet and it never kicks hounds when the Huntsman is looking. It gallops on, it jumps fences alongside and often in front of, horse-sized animals, it goes out of its way, sometimes literally, to demonstrate before the admiring eyes of the top people that it is enthusiastic and that its nature is so sweet that it can be ridden by any *competent* pony person. Only *you* know that its favourite sport, when the Huntsman, or anyone else of importance, is not looking, is booting hounds as far as possible; only you know it has a mouth like iron; only you are uncomfortably aware that it frightens you almost out of your wits because you know what it *can* do to you if you don't give it exactly what it wants to eat whenever it wants to eat it. It has you, so to speak, in the hollow of its tiny hoofs, because it will make you look as if you really are incompetent and scared stiff (which it has long ago convinced you that you are) unless you do its bidding at the toss of its mane. This blackmailing type is well aware that you daren't sell it because everyone who has seen it on its best behaviour will assume it is too good for you. The only thing you can do is to grow out of it by getting too heavy for it. Between ourselves, that is the reason for some of the overweight pony people there are about the place these days.

Grow out of it by getting too heavy

5.Taking care of Your Pony

AN EXCELLENT maxim is 'if you don't take care of your pony, your pony won't care for you' and as the pony almost always turns out to be the boss, it is worth remembering. It ought to have been an old Arab proverb and probably was before we thought it up. It should be nailed to the wall of every pony person's loose-box and above the bed of every aspiring pony person. Parents, too, might be glad to have it as a Christmas present to pass on to their young instead of the pony they were expecting for Christmas.

It is not unusual for ponies in the British Isles to live out of doors most of their lives, only being brought inside when there is a blizzard or something they ought to see on the television. It entirely depends upon what the pony is required to do to make some effort to earn its keep. If it is one of the craftiest types which has so organised its life and the lives of the humans it owns that it dictates the programme for the day, it will decide for itself whether or not it wishes to come in at night. If it has a liking for a certain

Its expression will become quite human

37

programme on the television, it will move in and sit on the sofa, when its expression will become temporarily quite human, until it decides it is bored, after which it will be safe for the people it owns to come downstairs again.

If, on the other hand, it is just an average unsophisticated and non-crafty type, it will expect to live outside the house but, nevertheless, in the best possible conditions, whether in a loose-box or in a field. If it is a thoroughly hairy sort which is allowed to wear its fur coat all through the winter, it may be much happier out of doors, so long as it has a shelter into which it can go to play cards

with other ponies and hatch plots for the discomfort of the humans with which it may have to consort next day. If it is a semi-sophisticated sort with a superiority complex and a non-furry coat (it is interesting that furry coats among ponies are regarded as a non-status symbol while, in many parts of the world, the reverse is the case so far as humans are concerned), it should either be fitted out with pyjamas in the form of a rug or should have its own bedroom in a stable. Most ponies prefer a loose-box to a stall because, whereas in a stall they are tied up and only have the wall to look at and are therefore likely to think the nastiest things about humans all through the night without getting anywhere, in a loose-box they can walk about a bit and practise kicking and bucking and biting from all angles. It is much easier to hatch plots when one has the freedom of movement to rehearse performances.

Ponies got along very well when they were just wild native ponies without humans to act as their slaves, but, ever since Pony Persons were invented, ponies have needed Pony Persons to look after them. It is, consequently, absolutely logical of ponies to demand the best possible treatment from humans. Whether they live out or in, they must now have the full first-class hotel treatment, complete with hair-dos, pedicures and a regular wash and brush up. They are not to be encouraged to leave their dirty shoes outside their bedroom doors, but the most sophisticated of them are inclined to do even that.

Feeding is an important part of the care of your pony. All ponies eat and some ponies will eat anything upon which they can lay their teeth. Original Pony spent most of its life grazing its way across a prairie and then grazing its way back again, like a lawn-mower on hoofs. After it had decided to team up with Man it came to the conclusion that it needed more and better food. One day, an early type of pony must have wandered into a field of oats grown by an early type of man who had stopped growing the wild variety, probably because he had married. The pony felt pretty good after its oat meal and from then on ponies have been demanding the

Excess energy

stuff on the menu. Some ponies get rather peculiar if they are fed too much oats and get full of the idea that they are the bosses of the human race, and, while all ponies know this, only the type who cannot hold his or her oats makes it obvious immediately a human sits on its back. The really cunning oat-full pony, however elated it may feel, takes the greatest possible care to avoid any direct evidence that its behaviour is connected with its food, suppressing its inclination to buck, bolt or otherwise get rid of its rider, until the latter has forgotten how much oats it has had. An experienced pony person can tell, by such small signs as whether the pony is muttering to itself or even giggling a little, as they set out, whether the creature can take its oats or not. There is a lot of protein in oats and it must be remembered that too much protein in a diet can lead to over-heating of the blood, excess energy and general misplaced enthusiasm.

Because the original ponies ate grass, it has become the custom to feed ponies hay, as this provides the necessary bulk food. Too much hay, like too much grass, produces bulky ponies if the pony is a glutton, and if you have a new pony you will soon find out whether your pony can take a lot of hay without becoming haystack-shaped. Most ponies can eat as much hay as parents can afford, but ponies, like parents, suffer from indigestion and the greatest care must be taken to avoid stuffing the animal with a rich and mixed diet before it takes part in a public performance of any kind. A pony with hiccups, to take the mildest example of what can happen, can be a considerable embarrassment at a Meet. But if you don't know how to feed your pony, do consult the nearest genuine expert. This will probably be the pony person next door whose little darlings get over the fence during the night and thrive on your parents' petunias.

As everyone who has ever ridden a sleepy type of pony will know, ponies can sleep standing up. This is a great disadvantage at gymkhanas and pony trials and hunts and other activities where the pony is meant to be being active. It couldn't matter less at the times when pony owners are themselves asleep in their own beds, but it does seem rather odd that pony experts insist that, whether they sleep standing up or not, ponies who live in stables must have bedding. There are, declare the pony-bedding experts, several kinds of pony bedding, including straw, peat moss and sawdust, but the most usual at the moment is straw. With the now almost universal use of the combine-harvester in the countries with advanced agriculture, straw is much shorter, literally, than it used to be, and this is obviously one of the reasons for the increasing number of shorter ponies in advanced countries. In the old days of long straw and short ponies it was not unusual for the old Head Groom to lose the Young Master's pony for weeks among the heaps of straw in the Young Master's pony's special loose-box and, with any luck, the Young Master himself. Today, in Britain, at any rate, Young Masters, long straw and old Head Grooms are all extremely scarce. It is thought, by the more optimistic pony people, that Old Head Grooms might come back one day.

Confirmed bed-eater

The trouble about bedding is that many ponies are inclined to eat it and some of them are such confirmed bed-eaters that they will eat any kind of bedding they can lay their teeth into, including mattresses if they manage to sneak into the house. The most reliable way of deterring them from bed-eating is to spread something on the bedding, such as mustard or pepper—that is if you have no objection to sleeping on mustard or pepper.

Grooming is an essential part of the care of the pony. The first stage consists of merely cleaning the animal, removing surface mud and dust and, if you own one of the shaggy sort, chasing out the bats and moths that tend to lurk in its coat. Grooming for condition, complete cleanliness and general showing off, however, involves at least three-quarters of an hour of hard work during which you must use the dandy brush, the body brush and straw wisp—in

Grooming from the other side of the loose-box door

turn, of course, not all together, unless you are proposing to hold one of the things in your teeth. The whole secret of successful grooming, it has been said, is to stand as far away from the pony as possible and hit it as hard as you can. The reference is to the proper use of the body brush, it must be explained to the uninitiated, and on no account, however badly the pony may have treated you, must you use a club.

A high proportion of pony owners are only too pleased to stand as far away from their ponies as possible and, one suspects, from the appearance of their ponies, groom them from the other side of the loose-box door. After all, some ponies can hit back much harder.

6. Gymkhanas and Shows

ONCE YOU have learned how to acquire a pony, look after it and even more or less ride it, it will be your ambition to compete in gymkhanas and rallies and pony shows and all that kind of thing. If it isn't, it jolly well should be, as your jolly District Commissioner or Area Manager or someone will tell you. Hacking about the lanes or even in the national parks or up and down the High Street (to show you can ride) is all very well, but you will never be considered a qualified pony person until you have at least had a good hard bash at someone in the potato race or jumped on a steward in the junior jumping. There is no need to be shy about it and certainly no reason to be snooty. Remember, as you gaze at

Your M.F.H. too, was probably once a Pony Club person

your local Master of Foxhounds, that it is more than likely that he, too, was once a Pony Club person and leaped heartily up and down in a sack in the sack race. The harder you gaze at him the harder it may be to realise this, but it is quite likely, all the same.

And so, appreciating what heights you, too, may one day reach, enter into the spirit of the good old British gymkhana with gusto. It is also helpful to take along, not only a pony, but a few shillings from your parents to pay the fees for the events as well. Upon arrival at the ground, you should instruct your parents, or any

43

other aged relative you can grab, to hold your pony for a minute or two. You should then proceed to the refreshment tent to fortify yourself with whatever may be the most popular form of refreshment for pony people of your age group. While doing this you will be able to have long sporting chats with your contemporaries who will, of course, have handed over their mounts to *their* aged relatives. These are not wasted moments, as you must hasten to point out to your pony-holders, when you decide to return to them, for, as anyone who has qualified in ponycraft knows, it is important to study form and to find out whether that ghastly girl on the odd-coloured pony has entered for the egg-and-spoon, under 13 hands and 14 Summers, it being an established fact that, however ghastly and odd the combination may be, it does win egg-and-spoons with sickening regularity.

Eavesdropping may be rewarding

Having thus fortified yourself with, presumably, soft drinks, and equipped with information more or less straight from the pony-owners' mouths (at this point must be mentioned with some diffidence, and considerable regret, that not all young pony people are strictly honest about the information they pass on in the refreshment tent to those pony people who are obviously in the beginners' stage and, therefore, a bit of eavesdropping may be even more rewarding), you should return to your pony. If it has not become bored and taken your aged parent home by the scruff of the neck, you should take it round to the appointed place for the start of the first event you wish to enter. At many pony gymkhanas and shows, entries are taken on the ground by stewards who have been trampled underfoot.

Meeting people you don't like in the Bending Race

A vast number of events has already been invented for gymkhanas, and more are being thought up all the time, the most ingenious inventors, one suspects, being people who would rather like to get their own back on other people, in the most sporting way possible, it need hardly be added. But let us take the simplest events likely to be encountered at gymkhanas and offer a little simple advice to the pony person who has already learned Ponycraft and is the possessor of a Crafty Pony. In the Apple Ducking, which involves riders dismounting and picking apples out of buckets with their teeth, a crafty pony can be of tremendous help, either in using its own teeth to extract your apple or in using its heels to discourage your nearest rival in using his or her own teeth. The Bending Race, which has long been one of the most popular of gymkhana events and necessitates riders galloping down a line of posts, passing them on alternate sides, turning round the last post and returning the same way to the finish, provides great opportunities for meeting the people you don't like at the right time on the wrong side, with often exciting results. The Obstacle Race offers wonderful chances of bumping into the most unlikely characters, and the Gretna Green Race and the Pair Relay Race

45

often have the most surprising results. But our advice is, whatever the competition, just leave it to the pony.

Gymkhana events are only a part of the modern pony people's annual plot to lure more and more non-pony people into their hay-net, so to speak. There are shows and rallies at which the ponies and riders are tested on their conformation and ability, rather than just on their cunning, as at gymkhanas. Even if the judges at these shows and rallies are under the impression that they are making their awards on ability, experienced pony people and their ponies know that, here again, ponycraftiness can play its part.

Take classes for the best riding pony, for example. Your pony may be a superb performer and, in its and your opinion, a good-looker as well, but you may also be aware at the back of your mind that it has 'nothing in front of the saddle'. Just in case the book happens to be read by an aged relative of a pony person who is not himself or herself a pony person, it must be made clear that the expression does not mean that the pony has lost its head. It means that its withers, its shoulders and all that, are not as evident as they should be. A really crafty pony person can disguise a pony's tiny faults in conformation by sitting slightly forward, pulling up the leathers a hole of two or letting them down a bit, or sitting rather farther back than usual. Care has to be taken not to sit too far back or you will fall right out of the back.

All qualified Pony Club judges will know these tricks, of course, not because they have tried them themselves, but because they have read about them somewhere. But you might get away with it at an unofficial show, such as the one you persuade your parents to run for yourself and your friends, especially if the judges are, by sheer coincidence, business friends of your father's.

Apart from the conformation problem, there is the matter of good ponycraft in going round the ring in such a way that you appear to be in full control of your pony. Even the nastiest ponies can, by means of bribes and promises, but never by threats, be persuaded to appear to be under control. The threats, in fact, are often made by the pony. At the first sign of gnashing teeth or the feeling that your pony's back is being just a little bit curved, like a bow from which you may be shot to come to earth you know not where, you must give it something to eat. Pony people who have pocketsful of carrots and sugar are often amazed how well their ponies behave—until the supply runs out.

And then there is the matter of Show Jumping. It is thought by some quite ordinary pony people who are quite happy riding their ponies around the countryside, that they can be accepted as absolutely genuine people without taking part in any sort of show jumping. It depends to some extent whether they live in the same district as a top show-jumping person, but, if they want to be thought of as even serious-minded pony people, they should, at least, put up a few striped poles in the paddock or the back garden, within view of all the neighbours who only know about horses and ponies through their television screens. It is not absolutely essential to jump the poles but, in suburbia and near-suburbia, in particular, it is advisable to have them around the place to prove that you know what ponies are for. Real show-jumping people don't have to bother about having striped poles about the place as status symbols, because they just don't care what the neighbours are thinking, anyway.

Nevertheless, all pony people should have at least some idea about show-jumping and the best place to start is your local show. You will soon find out whether you and your pony are cut out for the job and you need not worry about the little dear coming to any harm. He will go round, or through, if he doesn't like the look of the jump. You, on the other hand, are almost certain to go over it—do remember not to let go of the reins—and it's all experience which may be valuable to you in the hunting field later on, isn't it?

Remember not to let go of the reins

7. The Hunting Pony

As was mentioned at the beginning of this book, the pony was hunted by Man for pony stew in the days before Man was civilised by ponies. Ever since ponies made men their slaves, they have agreed to take humans hunting in return for large quantities of food, free accommodation and the best quality clothing. Nearly all ponies are keen on hunting but some are keener than others, and the only way you can find out into which category yours will fit is by taking it hunting.

Many of the best instructional books on ponies and horses have contained a chapter on a fictional day's hunting and in this chapter we have an account of a day's hunting which the uninitiated may find instructional and the experienced, we fear, may find rather nearer the truth than they dared to tell Father and Mother at the time.

Let us assume that you have arrived at the Meet. It is to be hoped that you have done so by the old-fashioned method of getting Mother out of bed very early in the morning (fathers, if they hunt, are fully occupied with their own horses, and their own thoughts for the day, and if they don't hunt, mutter under the bedclothes that they wish all the females in the house would stop bashing about the place at an unearthly hour) and that you are hacking to the rendezvous, instead of going by car and pony box. For one thing, getting Mother out of bed at an unearthly hour is much more fun and, for another, you can commune with Nature and watch wild life and study agriculture and all that from the back of your pony as you hack along. You can also practise staying on the pony's back.

At the Meet you should, as a beginner, tuck yourself and your pony into some quiet, out of the way corner, such as the bottom of a deep ditch or behind a barn, in order not to get in any of your superiors' (this means your elders') way and in order not to give your pony a chance to kick hounds. It is also good practice for avoiding the Secretary or other important hunt people who come round asking for money, as Mother will have explained to you. Pony Club people never hide away at Meets because, for one thing, they have a Special Arrangement about paying and so if you are a Pony Club person you won't have to hide either. Nevertheless, it is a good idea to practise not being noticed at Meets, in case you find you get yourself noticed too much later on.

Tuck yourself into some quiet corner

As soon as the Huntsman or the Master—it is often the same person these days, partly because it saves money and partly because a Huntsman is always considered to be of a higher status than a non-horn-blowing type of Master (the do-it-yourself idea having spread even into top field sports)—blows a toot on his horn, all the hounds will move off.

If they are not talking so much that they haven't noticed, the field, which means all the people on horses and ponies and a long column of people in cars as well, will move off, more or less in the same direction. Some of the cars will move off in both directions, which can be highly entertaining but is not your concern. You have many years to go before you reach the status of a car follower and can talk of all the fast hunts you have enjoyed on horseback. Anyway, all the best car followers who talk like that have come from other hunt countries and wouldn't dream of being seen on a horse in the country to which they have retired; not even hacking about.

And so, keeping modestly in the rear, you arrive at the first covert. If your pony is really enthusiastic about hunting you may

It is not a good thing to arrive before hounds

arrive, not in the rear, but before hounds, and unless your parents
are on very good terms indeed with the Master, this is not a good
thing. You must sit as quiet as a mouse while hounds are drawing,
listening intently to what each hound is saying and trying hard to
ignore what the real hunting people all around you are saying
about each other, particularly if it happens to be the day after the
Hunt Ball.

Hark! A hound speaks! Or is it Mother who has managed to
sneak up on you to give you more advice? No, it's a hound—there's
Mother still struggling across the plough to get at you. Another
hound speaks and then all the hounds start speaking at once, trying
to make themselves heard above the sound of the car followers
away in the lane, disagreeing with each other about the line the fox
is likely to take. The Master tells everyone to stop speaking, except
hounds and Huntsman, especially as he happens to be the
Huntsman himself. Apart from the music of hounds crashing about
in covert and the car people crashing their gears in the lane, all is
peaceful over the countryside.

Suddenly the Huntsman blows the joyful notes of the 'Gone
Away!' which you will instantly recognise, of course. One way of
doing so is by noticing that everyone is galloping madly after
hounds, but this is not entirely reliable because some hunting
people these days are not very good at knowing hunting calls and
tend to gallop madly about when all that the Huntsman is trying
to convey is that he wants the hunt terrier brought up, please.

Mother struggling across the plough

You will now go away with everyone else, whether you like it or not. Your pony will see to that and—oh good! You're going away just before Mother gets to you! You were not to know she still had your sandwiches. Cram on your hat, not too hard unless you'd rather not see where you are going, and SIT DOWN AND RIDE! That may seem to be a somewhat unnecessary instruction but it is a perfectly correct and much-used horse-person term. Riding that way is more comfortable, anyway.

This a moment you will remember for the rest of your life. It is quite remarkable how frightening experiences stay engraved on one's mind but, like all other hunting people, you will soon learn to talk about experiences being exciting but *never* frightening. Anyway, after the first few minutes, if you are still with your pony, you will be much too occupied staying with it to be frightened.

What an amazing sensation it is to be in the first flight on your first hunt—even if you meant to be at the back! All round you are galloping hoofs, belonging to other people's horses and ponies. Your gay little mount strides over the grass, and there is a feeling of power behind the saddle. It is the Huntsman. Get out of his way, for goodness' sake, or you may not be asked to come again. With a light touch on your rein, using both hands if the pony is keen, you do so. As the Huntsman passes you he calls out a cheery greeting, or something, and the world is yours. There is a rush of pure, clear air in your face and a cloud of hot, not so pure, breath down the back of your neck. It is the Colonel on his 17-hand ex-point-to-pointer, which, from the faint smell of brandy, was given a couple in its horse-box on the way to the Meet.

A feeling of power behind the saddle

There is green turf beneath the pony's feet and lumps of it flying up in your face. In the valley below, hounds are streaming along, and a field ahead of them is the brown dot that is the fox, and a couple of fields ahead of the fox there is a long coloumn of cars speeding along the lane. The car followers are anxious to tell the Huntsman which way the fox is going. You spot Mother's car in the lead and it is clear from the agitated way in which she is taking the corners that she is anxious to get into touch with you again to give you some urgent advice.

All this has happened in a matter of seconds, and suddenly you realise that you are approaching your first fence. It looms up, terrifyingly large, a strong-looking post and rails. There is an exhilarating feeling as it disappears from sight beneath the pony's ears. This is a pity (you really should have gone through the gate like everyone else) but someone will put it together again and the Hunt Secretary will explain the normal procedure on the telephone to your parents in the evening. And so on you gallop, convinced already that there is no sport to equal fox-hunting and no creature in the world so bold as a pony. Dismiss from your mind any

Someone will pull it together again

fleeting thought that you would prefer it not to be quite so bold, or that it would be nicer if it had been fitted with brakes. All ponies have brakes, but the difficulty is in finding where they are, and the less expensive the pony, all expensive-pony breeders will tell you, the harder it is to find them. The top and expensive-pony breeders spend a lot of time putting, not only brakes, but also gears and other devices into their ponies.

Having got through the first fence, you may well find that hounds have checked and you must explain to your pony that it is meant to stop galloping about, and to other members of the field that you are trying to explain this to your pony. With any luck, hounds will soon pick up the line again and off you go once more. By this time the young rider should have some idea what it is all about, in which case the young rider who has been trained by Pony Club instructors will be well advised not to say so to the elderly hunting people present who are too old to have the benefit of Pony Club training.

Another fence looms up (fences should always loom up in hunting literature) and the pony sails merrily over the gap left by the Hunt Secretary. There is now a screaming scent, hounds are in full cry and your cup of happiness is full to the brim—the

topper-upper being due to the fact that you have just galloped past
your most hated rival at Pony Club Camps and, even more so, at
Hunt Balls, screaming and in full cry upside down in a particularly
noisome ditch.

This is the life, you think to yourself, as the now gale-force wind
brings tears to your eyes and you gallop on and on, chiefly because
you can't stop the little brute. There is another check and then you
are off again. Pick yourself up and get back in the saddle. The
whole of the County seems to stretch before you in the glorious
sunlight. This is probably because your pony can't quite keep up
with the County. But never mind, there must be an awful lot of
ordinary people behind you, not forgetting that girl in the ditch.

If after a couple of hours, you are still more or less in the saddle,
you have done very well indeed for your first hunt. By this time
you will undoubtedly have lost hounds, lost your sense of direction

Tell her what grand sport she missed

55

and lost your way. The great consolation is that you will also have lost Mother and, as it will probably take you hours and hours to get back home, you will have plenty of time to think up the most blood-curdling account of the day's activities en route.

As soon as you arrive, make sure that Mother grooms and feeds the pony and puts it to bed as efficiently as you would have done yourself if you hadn't been too tired. There would be no point in asking Father. Then ask Mother how on earth she managed to get lost and finally, make a point of telephoning the girl you last saw down in a ditch and telling her what grand sport she missed. If she is in hospital, tell her Mother. If you do all these things you are already well on the way to being a first-class hunting person but, don't forget, you could never have done it without your pony.

8.The Holiday Pony

IT IS almost certain that, in the opinion of most ponies, they should all be on holiday most of their lives, although, they would add, if you asked them, even walking about in paddocks eating the grass down is hard work and is doing a lot of good for a lot of people, free of charge. But the more humane and intelligent pony owners will realise that ponies do appreciate a change of scenery and diet. It is therefore kind—and adults who have to keep their family's ponies around the place most of the year will be the first to agree —to move them elsewhere occasionally. The best way, parents will almost fall over themselves to agree, is to put the ponies on someone else's land.

A four-legged bathing raft

Making a weak place in the next-door paddocks so that even the laziest and fattest pony can get through to enjoy the next-door grass and scenery will, unless the neighbours are ridiculously unobservant, allow the pony to have only a brief holiday.

The ideal plan, from the owner's point of view, if not from that of the animal who would prefer to be left alone with lots and lots of lovely food and no work at all, is to take the pony with you and

57

persuade it to carry you about, admiring the view and acting as a four-legged bathing raft. Unfortunately, the majority of parents and ponies are unenthusiastic about this idea and, although some kindly farming people who do a little harvesting of holiday-makers, as well as the normal agricultural sort, are willing enough to provide board and lodging for equines in addition to humans (they find most of the former rather tidier in their habits than most of the latter), the average hotel does not approve of ponies on the premises and the most pony-minded of them will not allow them in the bedrooms in case they snore. Ponies are not popular on cruises or encouraged on coach tours, and so one has to face the fact that ponies, on the whole, have to be left behind.

For the really keen pony person there is, fortunately, a happy solution. If they cannot take their own ponies with them, there are plenty of holiday ponies available all over the country as well as Abroad. It is with British Holiday Ponies that we are concerned in this chapter and as the British have, during recent years, redis-covered the use of the pony for carrying them about—the loss of the use of their legs since the horseless carriage became a necessity for travelling farther than a hundred yards has probably had something to do with it—Holiday Pony Centres have sprung up all over the place.

Holidaying on a pony is known as Pony Trekking, presumably to distinguish it from just ordinary pony riding, which is fair enough as you don't even have to be an expert pony rider in order to take part. The ponies and the other characters in charge will soon make sure that you find out and, it must be stressed, the greatest care has been taken to ensure that all the recognised trekking centres are properly run and that none of the trekking ponies suffer. If the holiday-makers suffer it is their own fault for not looking where their pony is contemplating putting them.

It has been said that there is more jollity and mirth in a trekking holiday than is to be found in any other form of equestrian exercise, as any inexperienced trekking person whose accommoda-tion for the night has been within neigh-shot of the pony stables will have to agree. The ponies can sometimes be heard laughing so much that they roll in their stalls as they discuss the day's events.

Fortunately, inexperienced trekking people are not likely to understand pony language, especially if it is in Welsh Mountain, Dartmoor, Exmoor, Highland, Irish or, as is often the case these days, in Arabic-Thoroughbred-British-Native-Pony-cross dialect. It need hardly be stressed that the ponies at the trekking centre at which you have booked your pony holiday, from the approved list, of course, will not be so bad-mannered as to make rude comments

The ponies can be heard laughing

on the guests, so long as you have slipped your pony a secret carrot or a lump of sugar or two. It is also appreciated that no reader of this book would give any pony anything to giggle about.

But, as all the owners and staff of all the really efficient trekking centres will admit, there are still some trekking centres which are not quite as good as theirs, and they will at once recognise the ones we mean and will take note that none of the observations here could, by any stretch of imagination, be meant to apply to them.

And so let us assume that you will have arrived at a trekking centre in a wild, remote part of the British Isles, absolutely reeking with romance and dripping with legend, soaked in scenery, besotted by moors and mountains, where the air is like wine and, on a clear day, you can see the pony in front of you. What a change from the office chair, the seat in the train, the sofa in front of the television or even the back of your own pony, now stuffing itself in some sunlit pasture in the Home Counties.

The most notable difference may be that you are developing blisters much more quickly than you do on the office chair or the sofa, because the pony you are now riding keeps tilting either upwards or downwards. It has to, otherwise it would never be able to get up and down the gradients which you should have studied on your map before you set out, nor would it be able to cope with the contours which you should have studied before you demolished such a hearty breakfast. As the column climbs into the clouds you are aware that all around you are the mysterious calls of the curlews, the mewing of the mating buzzards, the barking of foxes and the plaintive cries, growing fainter and ever fainter, of one of the trekkers who leaned too far over to admire the valley and will, at any moment now, be arriving in it.

A trekker who leaned too far over

At the summit the leader calls a halt and the roll call. Satisfied that all the ponies are present, although some of them are no longer accompanied, he, or she, gives a brisk talk about the legend of the local highwayman whose mare was an ancestor of most of the ponies in the party, especially those being ridden by any visitors from Aborad, a short discourse on the wicked activities of the local smugglers, with a hint that the landlord of the inn at which the party is staying is a direct descendant of the smuggler chief, and a lurid account of the battle that took place during the 'Uprising' or 'The Border Trouble', or whatever may have been the most tactful period of history to mention in the area, on the moorland down below, of which one would have had a magnificient view if it hadn't been for the mist.

And so the happy party, full of the happy camaraderie of ponymanship and the keen air, the latter being described, by those members of the party who should never have come, as a 'howling gale', winds its way along and up and down and up and down until, tired but content, it dismounts, or in some cases, is lifted off, from its ponies and goes scampering, or staggering, back into the bar of the homely hotel. A drink or two, a bath, if there is one, and a jolly dinner of homely fare for those who can bear sitting down,

If it hadn't been for the mist

with much happy discourse about the day's activities: this is ponyship at its most primitive and best and is the pony person's absolutely ideal holiday.

You simply must try it, but do remember that, if you are sensible and select your trekking centre from the officially approved list, it won't be a bit like this description. On the contrary, there won't be any nasty clouds or beastly mist, nobody—well, hardly anybody—will fall off, and above all—most important—the ponies won't talk, whether you bribe them or not.

9. What to wear on a Pony

A PONY owner must have not only a great affection for his pony but also a great respect for it. This does not mean cowering under a heap of straw in a corner of a loose-box or climbing a tree in a paddock whenever it shows its teeth. It will be flattered by such reactions to its facial expressions, even if it was only intending to smile at the time, but the nastier-minded type of animal will be likely to regard them as a sign of an inferiority complex and follow it up by getting more of the upper hoof than it has already.

Respect, in the sense we have in mind, means treating the animal with dignity. A pony person who has recently been thrown may not be inclined to be respectful immediately upon recovering consciousness, but, upon reflection, will remember that the Horse is a Noble Animal and that it follows that the Pony must be only a hand or two less so.

They will also remember, in the intervals during which hospital visitors are not allowed, that, on the whole, Tootles, or whatever its name may be, was inclined to be more amenable if it had been given breakfast in bed, asked how it was feeling this morning and whether it wanted to go for an airing in the park, go hunting or kick something or somebody.

To respond to its wishes in this way may be regarded as respectful, by the pony, but, again, is likely to lead to pony blackmail. The best outward and visible sign of respect for the pony is the wearing of the correct dress when riding or driving it. There is an unfortunate tendency these days, partly due perhaps to watching television and noticing what peculiar riding clothes riding people on television wear and not noticing why they are wearing it, for such reasons as they are in the Wild West or being Cavaliers or Roundheads, to wear the oddest clothes on pony-back, under the impression that ponies don't care and don't even notice.

Ponies, on the contrary, are most sensitive and become acutely embarrassed if they have to appear in public carrying on their backs humans dressed in anything from shorts with bare legs to almost nothing with gumboots. They couldn't care less what their riders wear in private and, in fact, a pony with a really nasty mind and a rider it doesn't like very much is delighted to see that the latter is hatless, because it makes it so much easier to get rid of the latter for good on a nice hard road or against a lump of rock.

But all self-respecting ponies—and that means the lot—resent incorrectly-dressed persons riding them in places where they can be seen by ponies ridden by correctly-dressed persons.

There are degrees of correct dress, according to what your pony has decided it wants to do for the day. Young pony people can find all about what to wear from the people who sell the Right Clothes, but they may not be popular with their parents for doing so because the Right Clothes are expensive. If they have parents who once wore the Right Clothes, they should immediately take over whatever of the Right Clothing they can find in the wardrobes, cupboards, attics and stables in their homes. If they find that the clothes are in good condition and fit them and, above all, are not too out of date, they should immediately declare that they don't fit and are out of date and that they need a brand new outfit, just like their best friends at the gymkhana. This applies especially to pony people whose parents are always saying that they intend to take up riding again. They never will, of course, and are almost certain, under the threat of this sort of blackmail, to hand over the whole outfit without a murmur because this gives them an excuse not to take up riding again.

But the taking-over of parents' riding outfits is not always as

Your feet are smaller than Mother's

simple as it may seem. The young rider must bear in mind that parents who have once ridden are also not as simple as they may seem and nobody who has been in close association with the horse tribe can be entirely without cunning if they have survived long enough to become parents. Therefore, a little subtlety is often needed. For example, if you are a young woman who covets her Mother's boots, the line to take is that you fear your feet are rather smaller than hers and that, if you fell off your pony, Mother's boots would carry on, looking not only ridiculous in the stirrup irons all by themselves, but they would also be advertising the fact that Mother has big feet. This is an infallible way of getting either Mother's boots or, better still, brand new boots. The same applies to hats, caps and jackets. Sons who try the same methods on Father will find him a tougher proposition, much less likely to be influenced by insults about foot sizes.

Clothing experts and horse experts agree that the rider should wear the appropriate clothes for the sort of riding about to be undertaken. It would be absurd, they say, to wear hunting clothes if one is only going hacking or vice versa. They are absolutely right and beginners must not be put off if they happen to notice that some people in hunting clothes seem to be just hacking about. After all, they probably meant to go hunting when they started out.

The golden rule is to adapt your clothing to the pony you are riding—apart from adapting your clothing to the sort of riding you

It is unnecessary to wear a hairy outfit on a hairy pony

are doing. But even here there are snags and there is a danger of taking this sort of advice too literally. It is, for example, unnecessary to wear a hairy outfit just because you are riding a hairy pony, but, while it is not essential to be a beautiful golden-coloured girl with a fair, flowing mane if you happen to be riding one of those gorgeous Palomino ponies, it does help and, if you happen to be rather gorgeous yourself, may even be advisable.

A thin youth looks a bit odd on a fat cob, and a fat person on a slim, slinky Thoroughbred-type looks odder still, but this can be remedied to some extent by the feeding of a proper diet – to the rider, not the pony. There is no need to go to extremes in dressing to suit the colour of your pony, whether you are male or female, otherwise people who rode roans and piebalds and skewbalds would be likely to be stared at as they walked about in their roan, piebald and skewbald breeches and boots. On the other hand, they might just be taken to be modern young non-riding people, which would be much more embarrassing.

It has been rightly said that a well-groomed pony calls for a well-groomed rider. This does not mean that the animal will come round to the front door, all by itself, however well-groomed you may be. On the contrary, it is more likely to mean that it will stick its little hairy nose through the fence or over the loose-box door whenever it decides it needs your attention and call for you at the top of its horrible pony voice. However, it is true to say that a pony is likely to treat a well-dressed pony person better than it will a scruffy-looking one, probably because it thinks the former is better off than the latter and will keep it in the comfort it thinks it deserves. While it cannot be denied that some very weird pony people are to be seen wearing the weirdest and absolutely incorrect outfits at even the correct type of pony events, it must be stressed that it has been laid down, over the years, by top horse and pony people what all pony people, unless they don't mind being regarded as the absolute bottom, should wear. It is all very simple really, and the chief things to remember are that you should have a hat or cap at the top, and boots or shoes at the other end, the parts in between being covered as tastefully and economically as possible.

For hacking, which as every pony person should know already, means riding around the district for the purpose of exercising the pony, doing one's liver some good, demonstrating to other people in the district that you can ride a pony—or, best of all, all three—it is recommended that either a plain-coloured or tweedy sort of jacket should be worn, but on no account should anything that might be considered to be loud and horsey or pony adorn your person as it might frighten other people's ponies or give the impression that you are showing off, which is a bad thing, especially if you are. Breeches or jodhpurs (the latter were invented by horse people living in hot climates and are therefore immensely popular with the British, presumably because they live most of their lives in a cold climate) should also be worn as a connecting link between the jacket and riding boots or jodhpur boots. They are also helpful in making one's seat in the saddle more comfortable.

Both male and female riders ought to wear bowler hats, which were invented as crash helmets for horse and pony riders. One is, strictly speaking, incorrectly dressed if one doesn't wear a bowler on horse- or pony-back, and the business man who wears a bowler hat is equally incorrectly dressed if he goes to work without a horse or pony. As any erudite horse person will tell you, the bowler was made by a hatter named Bowler for William Coke, later Lord Leicester, because William's blood pressure suffered whenever his top hat, which was correct to wear in his day, fell off or got hung up in trees. Many horse and pony people look very smart indeed in bowler hats. They should fit well enough to enable the rider to see where he or she is going (eye-holes cut in them are considered rather unsmart, even in the more remote hunting countries) and must not be worn at Hunt Balls or Pony Club indoor social events.

If it decides to buck you off

Having stressed that hard hats absolutely must be worn, both for smartness and safety, it can now be revealed that many of the very topmost of horse and pony people are to be seen in the topmost horse and pony places wearing not only soft hats and caps, which are, in fact, approved by people who know all about riding clothes, but also head scarves. Soft hats and caps are usually worn by riders who have the misfortune to look like stage or film comics in stage or film dress, when they wear bowlers, but whereas soft hats and caps might give some protection if one has the misfortune to fall on one's head – as nearly every horse and pony person does sooner or later – a head scarf, even with the best possible designed ponies on it, will only make a really nasty-minded pony laugh itself into hysterics if it decides to buck you off.

The correct clothing for hunting varies according to the social or financial level a pony person has reached, and is apt to seem complicated. It, like most things in the pony world, is quite simple, once you know. The most reliable rule is to dress neatly and quietly so that you will not be remembered if you trip the Master up, kick hounds or wish to avoid the Secretary. For example, you should not wear a scarlet coat (incidentally, be careful how you describe the red-coloured coats that the most important or most expensive hunting people wear because, in many of the best and the worst circles these days, it is considered out-of-date or vulgar or quite wrong or not quite right to refer to 'pink', whereas not long ago it was considered to be absolutely the other way round and, therefore, your best bet is to wait until the other person, especially if he or she is older and more important than you are, says if first) unless you are getting quite old and important.

Once upon a time only Masters of Hounds and members of the Hunt staff wore caps, and then farmers were allowed to do so. And then members of farmers' families were allowed to do so. And then all young pony persons made it clear that they were jolly well going to do so. And then young pony persons who grew up to be horse persons did so, because they looked rather glamorous, or masterful, in caps, according to their sex. And so, any moment now, everyone who goes hunting, probably including the fox, will be wearing caps. And as most people, including foxes, look more glamorous in caps than they do in head-scarves, it might not be at all a bad thing.

There are, today, a number of different kinds of riding clothes for specialised riding occasions, such as Trials and Dressage and all that, but the guiding principle is to dress as well as your pony and this applies equally to the matter of hair styles. Once upon a time a well-bred pony could be distinguished from an ordinary sort, at pony shows, as much by its hair-do as by its conformation. Today it is not always so easy—and the same is true of riders. Hog-maned or otherwise neatly-coiffured ponies are sometimes to be seen carrying long-maned humans of indeterminate sex, and the judges have been known to complain, when the rider happens to be dismounted, that it is difficult to tell which is which. In the decadent days when young pony people wore shorter hair than their ponies, they often found that it was useful to be able to seize the pony by the mane when it was trying to get away. At the time of going to press the reverse is likely to be the case.

Long-maned human of indeterminate sex

10. The Pony's Point of View

IT SEEMED reasonable, having written a book about ponies, to consult a pony of our acquaintance, who refused to give its age but said it had no objection to being described as 'experienced', about its own views on the book and modern ponies and pony people in particular. The interview took place in the yard of an historic inn, somewhere in the West of England, in which thousands of horses and ponies must have snorted and kicked, rumbled and grumbled together as they waited outside, while their owners, farmer and hunting person, parson and highwayman (ponies not being particular about the sources of income or the morals of their owners) refreshed themselves, for at least four centuries. The pony and the place happened to be coincidentally convenient, because we happened to have persuaded the pony to carry us on its back into the afore-mentioned yard.

The pony remarked, as it shared our pint of beer, that it thought the book was a more or less reasonable account of the relationship between pony and human. It denied, however, the implication that ponies had taken over humans for ponies' comfort and gain but insisted, on the contrary, that ponies had taken over humans for their own good. Ponies, it emphasised, were not crafty. It was the humans who were the crafty ones and ponies were still trying to civilise them.

Ponies are still trying to civilise humans

While we were taking notes, the pony finished the pint and started to kick down the wall of the skittle alley. This, as the pony anticipated, brought the landlord out to enquire whether we required something else. We ordered two pints and the dialogue was resumed.

'About that first chapter,' said the pony, 'admittedly we got rather tired of being chased around the prairies and forests by savages in skins armed with spears and clubs, but we could have ignored them, you know.' The pony blew some froth across the yard and yanked a few wallflowers out of a tub with its long yellow teeth. 'The savages,' the pony explained, 'were so obviously under-privileged and lonely'—after all, they had only those half-witted dogs to keep them company in their primitive caves and forest huts, and everyone in the animal world was well aware that dogs only moved in with Man in order to take the best place at the fire and steal pies and things when Man wasn't looking. Whoever heard of a pony taking the best place in front of a fire? Besides, dogs didn't carry Man about on their backs although the pony had heard that some of the nastier-tempered ones had been known to carry Man about in their teeth, a thing no pony would dream of doing. Man was almost inedible, anyway.

The pony finished its pint and switched to cider. It reviewed several of the other chapters and was kind enough to remark that it fully agreed with some of our insinuations in the section on

British Native Pony breeds. We had, it regretted, made mistakes in the paragraphs referring to its own tribe but, of course, it added generously, we could not be expected to be right all the time and, being human, we just would not know that its own breed was the last surviving British Native Pony without trace of foreign blood —well, hardly any—since its ancestors walked across land that was now covered with sea water.

It insisted that we should stress that British Native Ponies were now going to Abroad places, such as America, in large numbers, in order to spread sweetness and light and to act as missionaries to those decidedly odd-shaped ponies who kept falling flat on their faces in Westerns on films and the television. British ponies, it said, never fell flat on their faces. They could even see the trip wires.

Falling flat on their faces

The pony took another bite of wallflower and munched it thoughtfully. 'That bit about hunting is fair enough,' it said. 'People just don't realise how much we ponies control the sport. One is always hearing a lot of propaganda about farmers being the only people who could stop hunting, but it never seems to occur to anyone that ponies could annoy the farmers so much by jumping on their crops that we could put them right against the whole thing. Those great stringy racehorses who come out hunting these days in order to qualify for Point-to-Point races don't recognise

73

A piercing neigh

which is the best crop to jump into when they see it. But,' the pony added hastily, 'we ponies wouldn't dream of doing such a thing unless we didn't like the farmer, or the M.F.H. or the person we were carrying about or we'd had enough hunting for the day and wanted to be sent home.'

The pony wondered if pony people ever considered what ponies thought of them. It was a great joke to put ponies into categories, but it did not appear to occur to humans that in loose-box and stall, field and farmyard, ponies might be rolling about almost helpless with laughter as they placed owners and riders into equally neat classifications. After a small bribe in the form of another glass of cider, the following comments on Pony Person types, as seen from the ponies' point of view were obtained. One would like to think they might be placed on the walls of all premises occupied by horse and pony people, if it were not for the thought that all those of us who have to have anything to do with ponies and horses might develop an inferiority complex as a result. But here they are offered in the hope that they may eventually produce a closer understanding between horse and human, pony and person, according to the pony interviewed.

The Highly-strung type of pony person, according to ponies, is often the good-looking (if female), by human standards, sort, with

It should bite the Beginner's parents

a tendency to bite and kick other humans on the evening before taking part in an important event, such as a horse or pony trial, show-jumping competition or even a day's hunting. They tend to become much nicer to their companions as the evening wears on and as they consume more of their liquid oats or barley or whatever their favourite food may be. At breakfast next morning—if they have any—they again tend to lay back their ears and kick or bite whoever may be nearest but, according to ponies, once in the saddle, they are often the nicest people a pony can hope to work with. 'The point being,' said the pony, 'that they, like ponies, are ultra-sensitive types, hence the mutual understanding.'

The Highly-strung type (female) often has good hocks and fetlocks, a thin skin and thrives best when brought in at night but should always be handled with care. Or so the pony said.

'*The Experienced* type of pony person,' said the pony, 'is to be regarded with some caution. One knows where one is with the obvious sort who usually has a thick skin, feathery fetlocks, a penetrating eye, a hard mouth and a piercing neigh. This type is always honest in that a pony can always tell when the type is likely to bite or kick because these actions are always preceded by the piercing neigh and, anyway, are nearly always directed at fellow humans. On the whole they are a popular sort of pony person

75

Pony Club meeting

among ponies, as they know about what ponies should eat and where they should sleep and so on.

'There is, on the other hand, another sort of Experienced pony person who cheats by not being obviously thick-skinned and not having feathery fetlocks and by neighing very softly. This kind can deceive the most experienced pony into thinking he or she has an inexperienced sort to deal with and the results can be most depressing for the pony. But, here again, although the pony will have to be polite to the pony person once it has realised it has been deceived and will have to make a quick switch over in its mental filing system, it can be sure of being properly fed and housed so long as it behaves itself. Experienced ponies and experienced pony people get along very well together as soon as each realises that the other is experienced.'

Ponies' club meeting

The Beginner is welcomed by the really nasty-minded pony but, our pony informant told us, he did not accept that any of this sort of pony still existed. 'Supposing they did,' he said, 'they might take advantage of the Beginner if the latter showed off by pretending to be an Experienced pony person. It would then be the pony's duty to demonstrate how much the Beginner had to learn and how foolish it was to show off, by, firstly, biting the Beginner, ever so gently and then, if pressed, by kicking the Beginner slightly, and finally, if the Beginner still refused to learn, by bucking him or her off—on soft ground, such as deep mud, of course.' Most ponies agreed the best way to make sure that Beginners realised that they had a lot to learn was by kicking or biting the Beginner's parents, ever so slightly, of course, to impress upon them that their offspring needed to be sent to an approved riding school. If the pony was convinced that the Beginner would never be worth living with, from a pony's point of view, it should bite or kick the Beginner's parents hard enough to convince them that ponies were absolutely beastly and on no account should be kept as part of the es- tablishment, not even as status symbols.

There were, the pony explained, as it finished the wallflowers, many sub-divisions of pony people and, for instance, ponies had a lot of fun placing them into pony-people breeds and, it added, with a scarcely suppressed snigger, ponies were highly amused by the fact that humans took so much trouble in sorting out breeding with regard to temperament, conformation, and performance of all animals except humans, these days. He supposed, he murmured, the point was that you couldn't sell humans, not even to other humans, any more and so it didn't really matter what their conformation and temperament, or even production, was like.

All that ponies bothered about was that pony people should get together to make sure that only the best types kept ponies, so that the best of the Beginners and the Highly-strung types produced the best Experienced types and so on. Anyway, he added, there was no doubt that it would not be long before ponies ruled the civilised world. It might not have yet come to the notice of the lay Press, but ponies had already taken over the British Isles pretty thoroughly, as well as many parts of the United States.

But, he remarked, he did wish people would stop assuming that ponies thought like humans and that they could talk and all that rot—animals only talked in Kipling and Anna Sewell and children's books and on the radio and would we please remember that he hadn't said a word.

The pony appeared to be thinking deeply and after a few moments of silence, asked for another glass of cider. We went in to get it. When we came out the pony had gone and as we trudged home there came across the hills the clatter of pony hoofs and the sound of what might have been pony laughter. Ponies will always win.